The Grandmother's Book

The Grandmother's Book

Joan Lowery Nixon

ABINGDON
Nashville

THE GRANDMOTHER'S BOOK

Library of Congress Cataloging in Publication Data

NIXON, JOAN LOWERY
  The grandmother's book.
  1. Grandmothers—Prayer-books and devotions—
English. I. Title.
BV4847.N58   248'.843   78-13621

ISBN 0-687-15681-5

Book Design by Linda W. Bryant

Photograph on p. 9 is by W. B. Witsell.

Photograph on p. 13 is by Ronald Benedict.

Photographs on pp. 25, 31, 33, and 37 are by Sid Dorris.

Photographs on pp. 2, 6, 21, 41, 47, 55, 59, 61, and 64 are by Bracey
Holt.

Scripture quotations are from The New American Bible © 1970 by The
Catholic Press.

MANUFACTURED BY THE PARTHENON PRESS AT
NASHVILLE, TENNESSEE, UNITED STATES OF AMERICA

This book is dedicated
to my friend

June Brush

as we share the joy
of being grandmothers to Melia

Contents

A Child Is Born

Our son-in-law, garbed in green hospital gown and cap, strides from the delivery room. The baby's a girl! he announces proudly. "They're bringing her into the nursery now! You can see her through the window!"

But I touch his arm, stopping him for an instant. "And Kathy? How is Kathy?" I ask.

He, with his youthful confidence in breathing exercises, natural childbirth, and highly recommended obstetrician, seems surprised. "Why, she's fine, of course," he answers. "She'll be out of the recovery soon, and you can see her." He hurries to join the group at the nursery window.

But his wife was once my baby—my first baby—and I had to know. I say a quick prayer of thanksgiving and scurry after him.

11

The nurse is holding up the baby for the grandmothers to admire. "Oh! I've seen that little face before!" I gasp, and I find I am laughing and crying at the same time for the wonder and joy of this tiny human being who is so much like her mother.

A little too late to be polite I turn to Kirk's mother and say, "I see so much of your son in her too."

But she is kind, and she squeezes my arm, laughing. "She looks exactly like Kathy," she says.

I notice that she is crying for happiness too, but the nurses are all smiles. I'm sure they are used to foolish grandmothers.

When I visit my daughter she is sleepy; so I tell her that I love her and that her baby is beautiful, and I have phoned her father and brother and sisters, and we are all rejoicing.

Driving home from the hospital I try extra hard to be careful, for I have had a heady experience, and I am floating. I am flying. I think of this new little girl with her rosy face and button nose and magnificently fashioned little fingers and toes. The world gleams; it glows. The color of joy must be gold. I have just seen one of God's miracles, and her name is Melia.

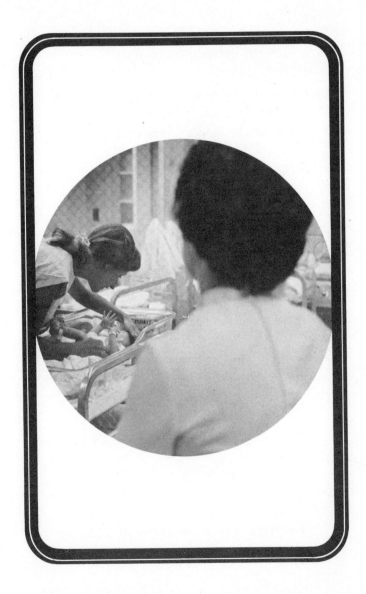

Yours, O Lord, are grandeur and power,
majesty, splendor, and glory.

For all in heaven and on earth is yours;
yours, O Lord, is the sovereignty;
you are exalted as head over all.

Riches and honor are from you,
and you have dominion over all.
In your hand are power and might;
it is yours to give grandeur and
strength to all.
Therefore, our God, we give you
thanks
and we praise the majesty of your name.
(I Chronicles 29:11-13)

Perfect Trust

I pick up my little granddaughter for the first time, my hands supporting her small head. I hold her close. It has been many years since I have held a new baby; yet instinctively the remembrance becomes a part of the present.

Her downy head nestles into the warm hollow of my neck as she makes the little kitten noises that will soon turn into loud demands to be fed.

Who I am, she does not ask. There are no questions in her mind as to what I am going to do with her. She trusts me implicitly, as she trusts the other adults in her life.

I can learn from this little one. As she trusts in me, so should I trust in God, asking no questions, relying on his strength to carry me through my lifetime.

How often I have given way to fears, to

doubts, to wondering if my prayers will be heard. How often I have lain awake in the dark, with only the small noises of the night to keep me company, and worried about things too trivial to remember now.

Her thumb is unsuccessfully trying to find her mouth, and she is letting me know it is time she be fed. I'll take her to her mother, and I'll try to remember this moment. Maybe by imitating her trusting ways, I can learn to relax with God in perfect trust, realizing how well he knows just what I need.

Your heavenly Father knows all that you need. Seek first his kingship over you, his way of holiness, and all these things will be given you besides. Enough, then, of worrying about tomorrow. Let tomorrow take care of itself. Today has troubles enough of its own.
(Matthew 6:32-34)

Thoughts
While Lying Awake
at Night

I am here to help the children with their new baby, but not in the middle of the night, they insist. They tell me I must not miss my sleep.

I lie in the darkness, smiling to myself, thinking of all the nights of interrupted sleep I have known because of hungry babies, or children with fevers or stomachaches or bad dreams, or even because of clocks that tick too closely to teen-agers' party deadlines.

My daughter and her husband are wanting to shield me from wakefulness at night, and they don't realize its familiarity probably makes it easier for me to get up with the baby than for them to do so.

I hear the hungry baby's cries suddenly stilled as she is put to the breast. The house is peaceful, and I remember those moments in the stillness

17

with my own babies. I never minded the nighttime feedings, because they gave me a few moments of undisturbed peace and communion between the baby and me. The many distractions of daylight hours were not there to bother us. There were only the two of us, alone and content in the quiet house—the two of us and God.

God seems closer when there are no distractions to interfere with our thoughts. How easy it was to forget his presence in the clamor of making hurried breakfasts, of getting poky children off to school, of rushing out the door with almost-forgotten lunch bags or sweaters or school books; doing the countless and never-ending chores that must be done around the house; hurrying to PTA meetings, to Little League ball games, to pediatrician appointments—

And where was God? He was somewhere among the clutter and jumble of my thoughts. Sometimes I tried to find him, but the phone rang or the youngest child cried, and the moment was ended.

But not at night. Not in the peaceful time in which baby needs mother, and mother needs God.

Sleepy? Yes, I was sleepy, but I never seemed

to mind. I wonder if my daughter understands these moments too. I think she will, in her own way.

> *Only in God is my soul at rest;*
> *from him comes my salvation.*
> (Psalm 62:2)

A Story About a Princess

The baby is content in my arms. She has eaten and has been wrapped snugly in a soft receiving blanket; and she is using the moments of wakefulness to study my face with eyes that are learning to focus. She is comfortable, nestled in the crook of my arm, because she feels loved and well cared for.

"I'll tell you a story," I say to her, and she watches me intently. "It's about a princess:

"Once there was a little princess with exactly the same name as yours. Her father, the King, and her mother, the Queen, decided to give a big party and invite all their friends in the kingdom so everyone could see and admire this beautiful, new little princess.

"And who should come to the party but twelve good fairies who oohed and ahhed and

said, 'Isn't she sweet!' and gave the princess the gifts of beauty and grace and charm and all the lovely things little princesses need the most.

"Then suddenly, in the doorway, appeared a very angry fairy!

" 'I wasn't invited to this party!' she shouted. She stomped to the princess' cradle, looked down upon her, and said, 'So to get even with all of you for this insult, this will be my wish: When the princess is sixteen, she will prick her finger on a spinning wheel and will fall into a deep sleep and will—'

" 'Oh, no, she won't!' The little princess' grandmother stepped up to the cradle, placed a protective hand on it, and stared right into the angry face of the bad fairy.

" 'What do you think you are doing!' the bad fairy gasped, and she grew so much angrier that her nose turned red. 'I am casting a magic spell, and no one can stop it!'

" 'I can stop it,' the grandmother said. 'Because I have some magic too, and my magic is stronger than yours is.'

" 'Ha!' said the fairy. 'Just what do you call your magic?'

" 'I call my magic "love," the grandmother said. 'My love is wrapped around and around the princess, and your spell can't get through it.'

22

" 'We'll see about that!' the bad fairy said, stomping her foot.

"But the grandmother continued to look the bad fairy right in the eyes until the fairy realized she had come up against a power much stronger than hers; and turning herself into a puff of smoke, she blew herself out the window and was never heard from again—"

She has gone to sleep before the story is finished, but I know that she got the message. Although her life has been measured only in a matter of days, each one of those days has been filled with love. And that's what counts.

There are in the end three things that last: faith, hope, and love, and the greatest of these is love.
(I Corinthians 13:13)

A Time for Comfort

Late in the afternoon, as the sun sweeps low in the sky, the baby is fretful.

"Don't worry," I tell my daughter. "Babies have their fretful times." And I think how interesting it is that even one so young should pick this low ebb in the day in which to do her fussing. Her mother is tired too; so the best thing I can do to give both of them comfort is to pick up the baby and rock her.

What gives a baby comfort? Since she is dry and fed, I hold her close to my chest as I rock her. She can hear the beat of my heart, which might be comforting in its familiarity, reminding her of a time just a few weeks ago when, within the sheltered womb, she could hear the steady heartbeat of her mother.

I softly sing a lullaby to my granddaughter, the words coming from a snug place in my

memory where they have been stored, rust free and mothproof, these many years, ready to be used again. I sing another and another. Although the quality of my singing is better left unmentioned, the baby doesn't complain. Maybe it's the words of love, maybe the rhythm, maybe the interesting vibrations she feels against my chest; but soon she is asleep.

On the sofa my daughter is asleep too. Wrapped in the warm, fleece robe that covers all but her bare toes, she sleeps as peacefully as her child does. I have to smile. I didn't know I was singing my grown-up daughter to sleep with lullabies too.

The room in the growing dusk is peaceful, and I think of how often we serve as the tools God uses in giving comfort. My daughter's soft cheek rests against the sofa pillow; her child's soft cheek is warm against my chest. Through God I have brought them comfort; and oh! how much comfort their love has brought to me!

Praised be God, the Father of our Lord Jesus Christ, the Father of mercies, and the God of all consolation! He comforts us in all our afflictions and thus enables us to comfort those who are in trouble, with the same consolation we have received from him.

(II Corinthians 1:3-4)

So Much to Learn

Our granddaughter is studying my face. I wish I knew what thoughts flicker behind those serious eyes. There is so much for her to learn. Is she telling herself this in some baby language of her own?

She is working right now on facial expressions. What is Grandma doing when she stretches her mouth wide like that? and when she says, "You can smile! Try it"?

And what does this little girl think? She must understand something of what I am saying and doing because a tiny crease comes into her brow; she concentrates deeply on what she is trying to do, and she ends up with a pleased expression. Not a smile, but the preliminaries to smiling.

Never mind, the smiles will come soon.

There is so much for her to learn, so much for those questioning eyes to discover. And this is just the beginning. She will spend all the years of her life in new thoughts and discoveries. May she always have the willingness to learn.

And may I have this willingness too. As a grandmother I hope I will never reach the point at which I think I know everything I need to know. I hope I will always reach out, learning from those around me, learning from my little granddaughter, and learning from God.

A wise man by hearing them will advance in learning,
an intelligent man will gain sound guidance,
That he may comprehend proverb and parable,
the words of the wise and their riddles.

The fear of the Lord is the beginning of knowledge;
wisdom and instruction fools despise.
(Proverbs 1:5-6)

Right Now, God!

When this baby is hungry she cries; when she is wet and uncomfortable she cries. There are variations in her whimpers and wails, and we get the message. She wants something done, and she wants it right now.

We hurry to meet her demands, because she cannot understand explanations. When she is a little older it will be time for her to learn patience, to discover there are moments in which one must wait for the things one wants and needs.

Patience.

This is a lesson most of us must learn in our very young years. How helpful it would be if we could apply that patience to God.

I find myself praying urgently for things I feel are so important to my life, and although I don't actually say, "And please, dear God, will you answer my prayer before noon?" the words might as well be there. I plan my life, I decide what I need, and then I practically shout, "Now, God, now!"

As the parents know what the child needs, so God knows what we need; and what we ask for doesn't always fit in with what we should have. Maybe, as I watch my granddaughter grow and learn that the development of patience is a necessary aspect of a happy life, I can grow and learn too—and apply my patience to my prayers, knowing that God has the final and the right answer, and—thanks be—has infinite patience with *me*!

The Lord does not delay in keeping his promise —though some consider it "delay." Rather, he shows you generous patience, since he wants none to perish but all to come to repentance.

(II Peter 3:9)

The Grandfather

My husband is holding his granddaughter so very carefully, his big hands grasping her firmly. She is content in his arms, as his own children were, sensing the strength and devotion that would protect those he loves from any kind of harm.

While she is studying him with her intent, ever-learning gaze, I am studying him too.

Once he sat in a rocking chair with our firstborn on his lap. He was young and slender, and his hair was red.

Now he sits in a rocking chair with his first grandchild; and time has added dignity, responsibility, and more than a few gray hairs.

Where did the time go between then and now? And why did it go so fast?

Once a teacher explained to our class that our

life-spans occupied but a fraction of a second in the whole scheme of eternity; and I wanted to shout, "Wait! There are ideas to explore, things to do, places to discover! Please give me more time than that!"

But time goes on relentlessly. My husband and I have come a long way together. We have tried to share with our children all that we understood of the excitement and wonder of living, the hope in each new day, the promise of God's love.

Maybe it's not such a distressing thought that my husband and I are growing older, because we have come this way together. And now God has added a new, exciting dimension to our lives. How lovely it is to be grandparents.

Grandchildren are the crown of old men,
and the glory of children is their parentage.
(Proverbs 17:6)

Make
a Joyful Sound
unto the Lord

The baby has learned to smile, and her smiles burst forth like holiday sparklers, lighting our hearts. Joy fills the room.

At what are we smiling? We don't know, and we don't care. We are communicating with one another in happiness, and the smiles are the outward display of our delight and our love.

God wants us to be happy. Christ told us that even while doing acts of penance we should put on cheerful faces. And happiness grows from the happiness of another.

This little girl will have moments in life when tears must come, and joy will be far from her mind. But the small, daily trials can bring glimpses of humor if she tries not to take them too seriously.

Even during the darkest of moments she will

find sources of happiness around her—in those who love her and want to share her problems as well as her pleasures.

And God gives us little bonuses of joy each day if we know how to look for them: a tiny blossom tucked into the leaves of the potted violet on the table; a bright green lizard on the windowsill, puffing his red-bubbled throat to attract a mate; a mockingbird's exuberant trill from the elm tree: gifts of joy, entwined with our lives, in proof of God's love.

I hope through the years I can provide some of the joy in our granddaughter's life. She has already given me great joy just through her existence. We can smile and laugh together and make a joyful sound unto the Lord.

A joyful heart is the health of the body,
but a depressed spirit dries up the bones.
(Proverbs 17:22)

Finding Time

She has set the pace, and the time is hers. For our granddaughter not a moment of her life is wasted. In her waking moments she exercises her small arms and legs, she studies the people and things around her as though she wants to fix all in her memory forever. When she is hungry, it is time to eat; and when she is tired, it is time to sleep.

As she gains value from each moment of her life, so too can I learn not to misuse the hours and minutes entrusted to me by God.

Perhaps this is one of the greatest benefits of being a grandmother. The Lord knows there were past hours I wasted that I could have spent with our children, hours in which I was "too tired" to read another picture book, "too busy" to share a happy moment. But I have been given a second chance with our granddaughter. Each minute is valuable; each minute a gift from God that we, together, can give to each other.

Are grandmothers more patient than are mothers? Are they less busy? I don't think so. I think that grandmothers, through experience, have learned the merit of each minute. Through the years ahead I hope to have many of these moments to share with this child, moments that will be precious because they are ours.

There is an appointed time for everything,
and a time for every affair under the heavens.
(Ecclesiastes 3:1)

Other Grandmothers

A few of my friends have grandchildren. They have brought out pictures of their grandchildren for me to admire. These pictures are usually tucked in special pockets in their handbags so they can be pulled out instantly when the conversation at the lunch table languishes.

I have seen and admired them. Sweet-looking babies. And I have nodded smiling agreement at the words of effusive praise for these nice babies' many accomplishments.

Now I look at my own grandchild, and for a moment my heart aches with pity for my friends whose grandchildren couldn't possibly measure up to this small and perfect baby. The wonder of her! The beauty of her!

I must remember to be kind.

I promise myself that my heart will be filled with charity and mercy, that I will look upon the pictures of the grandchildren of my friends and smile and agree to the verbal lists of their charms; and I will hug within myself the marvelous knowledge that of all the grandchildren of the world, mine is truly the most adorable.

Of course, I will probably brag a little bit. Grandmothers are allowed to.

Blest are they who show mercy;
mercy shall be theirs.

(Matthew 5:7)

A Need
to Be Prudent

My daughter and her husband have lots of ideas about child care, but so have I.

They keep a copy of Dr. Spock's book on hand. I like Dr. Haim Ginott and Transactional Analysis.

They tell me their ideas of child care and training.

I keep my mouth shut.

I remember so well when I was a new mother, delighted with my little daughter, but terrified that I would make mistakes that would cause traumas in her young life.

And yet I instinctively knew that my husband and I alone had been given this challenge, and we would accept it and make it our own. This was our child, we were her parents, and we

43

would do our best to give her a happy, productive childhood.

I know my daughter is a little frightened of this awesome responsibility too. I know our son-in-law is somewhat overwhelmed at the task set before him. But I also know this is a project they will work out together and will do a better, happier job if they don't get interference from a well-meaning grandmother.

I hope I will always remember that these young parents are the meat and strength and sustenance of the child. Grandmothers are the pastry that comes at no extra charge. And too much pastry isn't good for anyone.

A time to be silent, and a time to speak.
(Ecclesiastes 3:7)

You Want Too Much, Little Old Woman!

The baby begins to wake, and even before her eyes are open she has her fist in her mouth. She makes loud, slurping sounds that cause us to laugh. Is this her first attempt to use subtlety in achieving what she wants?

But hunger is a real thing to this little one, and her mother quickly feeds her.

Hunger for food—the first of the hungers that assails us.

I tidy the room, smoothing a sheet, folding a receiving blanket, glancing with a smile at my daughter with her child so content at her breast.

How many hungers we feed upon. As we grow we hunger for love, for companionship, for intellectual growth, for approval; and sometimes this hunger can expand in the wrong direction as we hunger desperately for success, for financial gain, for power, for so many material things.

Sometimes I think of the folktale about the old woman who saved the life of a magical fish and was granted a wish. But the more the fish gave her, the more she was back at the bridge calling, "Little fish, little fish! I have another wish!" Finally, the little fish, in exasperation, cried, "You want too much, little old woman!" And all the material things he had given her disappeared, along with the fish and his magic.

This folktale often comes back to me when I find myself hungering for something I really don't need, something not in the least essential to my real happiness. And I look in the mirror, shake my head at myself, and say, "You want too much, little old woman!" With the ludicrous fish in the folktale peering over my shoulder, the hunger is quickly abated.

At this point in my life I can see more clearly that aside from my basic needs, the only hunger worth satisfying lies within God, within this love greater than any other I could possibly know.

Yet the world is around me, and occasionally I have to remind myself, with an attempted stern look and a giggle, "You want too much, little old woman!"

Jesus explained to them:
"I myself am the bread of life.
No one who comes to me shall ever be hungry,
no one who believes in me shall ever thirst."

(John 6:35)

So Many Questions

As our granddaughter grows, she will ask so many questions: What holds up a bridge? What makes thunder? How does a flower grow? Where did I come from? If God is everywhere, why can't we see him?

When her mother was a little girl, old enough to write, I found her laboriously printing on a large sheet of paper, her pencil clutched tightly in her fingers, her tongue between her teeth, her forehead wrinkled in concentration.

"What are you writing?" I asked her.

"I'm writing a list of questions," she said. "Things I have to find out from God as soon as I get to heaven."

Our grandchild's parents, her teachers, her grandparents, her friends—all will try to answer her questions patiently and honestly, but

49

there are some things she will have to take on faith.

Faith for an answer is not a distressing thing. It can often make a more satisfying answer than one that can be given in concrete terms. When I tell this child "I love you," I cannot show her a single proof of this statement. She must take it on faith. But if she does, then the love becomes even more beautiful, even stronger between us.

And so it is with God. How contented I am when I say to him "I believe in you, and I believe your word," for this belief becomes a strengthened bond between us.

Sometimes, over the years, I have had doubts; but God has guided me to the answers. Sometimes I have found that the most beautiful answer of all is *faith*.

Just as you know not how the breath of life
fashions the human frame in the mother's womb,
So you know not the work of God
which he is accomplishing in the universe.

(Ecclesiastes 11:5)

Little Red Ridinghood -A New Version

Babies love to be talked to. Our granddaughter watches my face as though she is waiting for me to speak.

All right, little one. I'll tell you another story. It's about a little girl with the very same name as yours. But she always wore a little red cape with a little red hood when she went out to play; so everyone called her Little Red Ridinghood.

Well, one morning Little Red Ridinghood's mother gave her a basket of fresh apples and said, "Please take these across the park to your grandmother's house, and be careful along the way."

She put on her cape and hood and took the basket of apples and started across the park.

It was a sunny Saturday, and the park was filled with playing, laughing, happy children.

Little Red Ridinghood skipped along the path past the playground and around the lake and through the woods.

Just inside the woods she met a wolf who said, "Where are you going, little girl?"

Little Red Ridinghood had been watching Saturday morning TV cartoons; so it didn't surprise her at all to hear a wolf talk, and she answered, "I'm going to my grandmother's house to give her these apples."

"And which is your grandmother's house?" he asked.

"The pretty white house with the pink rosebush in front that is right across the street from the park," she told him.

That sneaky old wolf disappeared among the trees and rushed to Grandmother's house, where he knocked on the door. The minute Grandmother opened the door he pushed his way in and said, "I'm going to eat you up! And as soon as Little Red Ridinghood gets here, I'm going to eat her up too!"

"Not if my instructor in the "Self-defense for Women" class knew what she was talking about!" Grandmother said. And in a few minutes she had subdued the wolf and called the police, who came and took him away.

Little Red Ridinghood arrived with the

apples for her grandmother, stayed to eat one with her and to play three games of Fish and four of Old Maid. Then Grandmother walked with her back through the park and watched until she stood safely at her own front door.

The next morning Grandmother phoned some of her grandmother friends who had more time to do things than some of their busy daughters with their young children to care for; and they went to a city council meeting and made firm, grandmotherly noises until the city appointed a guard to watch over the children playing in the park. And the grandmothers took turns watching too. From then on, Little Red Ridinghood came to visit her grandmother often.

"What I am doing is sending you out like sheep among wolves. You must be clever as snakes and innocent as doves."

(Matthew 10:16)

A
Baby's First Steps

The days go fast, and this tiny girl, so new to the world, will learn to sit, and crawl, and finally try her first steps.

One of our daughters used great caution in learning to walk. She held to the edge of the chairs and low tables until she had thought each step through, then ventured forth. Another daughter tottered with reckless abandon across the living room to our waiting arms.

But both of them took many falls, teetering back and forth until they landed on diaper-padded bottoms.

"Come on," I would say. "You can do it." And I'd lend a hand to help them to their feet so they could try again.

Now, a little older, and I hope a little wiser through experience, I can see such a strong

parallel in my life with that of the child learning to walk. How many falls I've taken, and how seldom I've thought about God's encouragement being there, if I had just looked for it; his hand to take, if I had just reached for it. Step by step through life, there are bound to be problems that cause us to stumble, and sometimes those falls can be painful.

It makes it easier to realize now that I don't have to walk without help, that those aren't lonely steps I'm taking. I can have confidence in my journey when I recognize that I'm walking at the side of God.

You have been told, O man, what is good,
and what the Lord requires of you:
Only to do the right and to love goodness,
and to walk humbly with your God.

(Micah 6:8)

Through the Eyes of a Child

I'm going to love being a grandmother. Besides enjoying these new baby moments, I'm looking forward to the days ahead.

When our granddaughter is old enough, there wll be so many experiences to share. How awesome is the growth of a seed into a tiny green shoot with the promise of a flower to come. How strong under the hand are the muscles of the pony who waits for a young rider at the pony-ride gate. How breathless can be the high-speed ride of the horses on the merry-go-round at the park, and how exciting the baby animals behind the small-finger-and-nose-smudged glass window in the nursery at the zoo.

What a God-given blessing to be able to see the world again through the eyes of a child.

With each of our children it was a new experience, new questions, new ideas to be explored, new wonder in their eyes; and with our granddaughter it will be a new excitement shared in a new way.

It doesn't take long to learn that it is the simple things children love best; and their joy brings these experiences into the importance they truly deserve.

Sharing laughter and wonder and fun with children, seeing the world through their eyes, helps me to understand what is really important in life and what is not.

"I assure you, unless you change and become like little children, you will not enter the kingdom of God. Whoever makes himself lowly, becoming like this child, is of greatest importance in that heavenly reign.

"Whoever welcomes one such child for my sake welcomes me."

(Matthew 18:3-5)

Grandmothers Are for Spoiling

I'd like to spoil our granddaughter a little bit.

Oh, there are grandmothers who spoil their grandchildren, and grandmothers who *really* spoil their grandchildren, but they are two distinct and separate types.

Once, when our children were very young, I heard one of them say to a friend, "Grandmothers are for spoiling."

I knew what she meant. She was expressing that warm, delicate relationship between grandchild and grandmother in which the grandchild is made the loving recipient of extra caring, extra attention, and a few extra treats tucked in along the way—all solidly within the outside boundaries of the rules the parents have set.

To really love my granddaughter means I

must care enough to help her learn the rules her parents have established. They are working at being good parents, and a little sneaky sabotage on my part could only result in harming the relationships of all concerned.

So I'm not going to say, "You can stay up past your bedtime, but don't tell your parents." Instead, I'm going to make the hour before her regular bedtime one of happy sharing, with as many picture books to read as I can squeeze in.

I'm not going to say, "Surely you can skip your bath if you just don't tell anyone I let you." Instead, I'll provide some special bubble bath, or a bar of soap in the shape of a duck, and make it a time of giggly fun.

Oh, I may be tempted to break a few rules once in a while, but I hope I have enough good sense to remember not to. It's the parents, not the grandparents, who have the authority over the child; and that's the way it should be.

Let everyone obey the authorities that are over him, for there is no authority except from God, and all authority that exists is established by God.

(Romans 13:1)

The Grandmother of Jesus

This I know: Jesus had a grandmother, and her name was Anne.

But I wonder; When he was a baby, did she hold him on her lap and hug him and tell him tales to make him laugh? Did she kiss away the small bumps in his life and set him on his feet again? Did she pray for only happiness in life for her grandchild yet try to help prepare him for the trials that would come?

And did she love him with that special love that belongs only to grandmothers?

I think she did.

I think she was a good and loving grandmother, and I'm going to try to be that kind of grandmother too.

Then you will lead a life worthy of the Lord and pleasing to him in every way. You will multiply good works of every sort and grow in the knowledge of God.

(Colossians 1:10)